SOFT TACO MURDER

A Mexican Café Cozy Mystery

Holly Plum

Copyright © 2017 by Holly Plum

All rights reserved. No part of this publication may be reproduced, stored in or introduced into a retrieval system, or transmitted, in any form, or by any means (electronic, mechanical, photocopying, recording, or otherwise) without the prior written permission of the copyright owner of this book.

This is a work of fiction. Names, characters, places, brands, media, and incidents are either the product of the author's imagination or are used fictitiously. Any resemblance to actual persons, living or dead, business establishments, events, or locales is entirely coincidental.

CHAPTER ONE

"Why can't we just go to the beach?"

Mari Ramirez's younger brother Alex wrinkled his nose as he watched Mari unpack camping equipment.

"Well, that would have involved a longer drive, and you know how Dad feels about that," Mari replied. "He would rather vacation somewhere nearby where he can get back to the restaurant in a hurry if he needs to."

"We live near the Gulf coast," Alex continued. "There are plenty of beaches to choose from that are close enough."

"Dad would never go for that," Mari said as she unpacked a carrying case full of cooking utensils. "This is the farthest away he has been from the restaurant in years."

"Don't remind me," Alex responded. "Mom has been talking nonstop about that. If she comes across any more bugs, I think she might explode. You know how she feels about camping, but it is the only thing she could get Dad to do."

Mari and her family were spending a weekend in Tortoise Nation, a sprawling nature park in Texas Hill Country. On their way into the camp grounds an hour earlier, they had passed a bus full of teenagers from a church youth group on its way to Tortoise Lake, a popular tourist destination during summers and holidays. Seeing this, Mari had worried that the campground might be overcrowded. She'd been pleased when they arrived at their campsite to find it empty.

Mari had visited the campground a couple of times on student retreats in high school. She found the hiking trails lined with oaks and cedars a welcome change from the chaotic world of waiting tables at her family's restaurant. She loved hearing the songs of hundreds of different birds twittering together as if competing for recognition as she rose in the morning before dawn to climb Tortoise Hill.

"I hope you like tiny sausages and macaroni," said Mari's other brother, David, as he entered the tent carrying a sleeping bag on his shoulder. "Because that's all we're eating for the next three days."

"You'd think Dad would let us take advantage of the *many fine grills* available throughout the campsite,'" Alex said, mimicking the voice of the woman from the Tortoise Nation commercials.

"You would think," David replied, pulling off his thin hoodie to reveal a sleeveless t-shirt and a well-toned pair of arms. "But mom says he's supposed to destress while he's here. Apparently, the thought of us trying to light the grill and cook up some steaks stresses him out."

Alex rolled his eyes. "He ought to give us some credit. We've been running our own food truck for over a year now." David and Alex operated a taco truck in an abandoned parking lot on the edge of town every weekday during the lunch hour. Turning to Mari, he added, "Even *you* have to admit he's being a little ridiculous."

"He has always been this way," Mari said, swiping her chestnut-colored hair to the side. "And in his defense, hasn't your food truck been the center of more than one grease fire?"

"*Small* fires," David added, reaching into his gym bag and pulling out a pair of green and white ping-pong paddles. "It's no worse than the problems we've had at the restaurant—thieving employees, media scandals—"

"True." Mari took a deep breath. "Why don't we just try and enjoy our weekend in the great outdoors. I mean, what's the worst that could happen?"

***

Once they had finished setting up their tents, Alex and David led Marie's bulldog, Tabasco, into the woods while their father went for a quiet walk alone. Chickadees and cardinals stirred in the branches above them. This was too much excitement for the dog, who ran madly from one tree to another as if hoping he could scare the birds into flying down out of the trees and into his waiting paws.

While Mari waited for them to return, she and her mother worked together to set up the fire pit in the shade of the cedars that surrounded them.

"I know your dad requested that I don't do any work this weekend," Mrs. Ramirez said, producing an enormous bronze Dutch oven from beneath her sleeping bag. Mari got a distinct impression that she had been hiding it there. "But I can't resist making a few meals while we're here."

"Mama," Mari scolded her. "You know what Dad is going to say when he sees this. His shouting will be heard clear through Tortoise Nation."

Mrs. Ramirez shrugged. "I wasn't going to let us subsist on hot dogs and macaroni the entire weekend. I love your brothers, but their food isn't what you would call fine dining. I can't leave you to do all of the cooking."

Mari glared at her with suspicion. "What are you going to make?"

"It's an old family recipe," she said, removing two sealed packages of beef and a garlic salt shaker from inside her pillowcase. "My own Abuela used to make it when we visited your uncle out in East Texas. Trust me. You'll love it."

Mari clutched her stomach nervously. As hungry as she was, she had never been particularly fond of meals that consisted of throwing whatever happened to be hiding in her mother's luggage into a pot and letting it simmer. "Sounds great, Mom," she said in an unconvincing tone.

Mrs. Ramirez smirked shrewdly, choosing to ignore the lie. "Anyway, I know you haven't eaten today. By the time this is ready you'll be begging me for double portions."

Mari doubted this, but she didn't think it polite to say so.

As the sun began to set, Mari's brothers and their father returned to the camp site. To her surprise, a fourth man emerged from the back of their pickup—Officer Rick Kinney from back home.

"Hey you," Rick said, touching Mari playfully on the nose. Even in the gloom she clearly saw his boyish grin and too-large ears. Her stomach fluttered with apprehension. They had gone on several dates but never resolved whether they were *dating* or not, and she couldn't help wondering why her family had invited him on the trip without telling her.

"Hey," Mari replied. "This is a surprise."

"Is it?" Rick said with a look of confusion. "Oh, I see what's going on here."

"You do?" Mari raised her eyebrows.

"Your parents didn't tell you I was coming, did they?"

Mari shook her head, and Rick nodded. With his hands tucked in his back pockets, he tried to carry on like normal. "I can't wait to eat whatever your mom is cooking up for dinner. She's my favorite chef in the family. No offense."

"How do you know she is the one cooking?" Mari asked.

Behind them, Mr. Ramirez snorted. "If you really thought your mama was going to let you brothers cook dinner—well, you don't know your mom very well, that's all I can say."

Mari turned to her two brothers, who were already laying out plates and dishes. She had a funny feeling that they had threatened to make dinner in the hopes that their mother would intervene to make it for them.

The Dutch oven stew turned out to be much better than she had expected. As Mrs. Ramirez had predicted, Mari ended up eating it with relish and then asking for seconds. Mrs. Ramirez grinned as she slapped another portion onto her plate as if to say *I told you so*.

Mari wished she could relax in the company of her family, but it felt weird to be sitting around the fire pit with them, and the guy who might or might not be her boyfriend. The Ramirez family was awkward even at the best of times, and tonight was no exception. Mr. Ramirez told Rick a long, dull story about a shipment of chili beans he had received the other day instead of the black beans he had ordered. Rick listened politely and struggled to look interested. Meanwhile, on the other side of the pit, her two brothers engaged in an ongoing debate about the difference between a turtle and a tortoise.

Mari rose from her seat with a mortified feeling. She needed to use the restroom which meant that she needed to pee in the woods. But she didn't want to say that in front of Rick.

"I, um, need to go into the woods for a minute," she said, motioning to the trail that led out of the camp site. Luckily it was dark enough that no one could see her cheeks turning red.

"Are you sure you're okay?" Rick asked, half-rising from his seat. "Do you need someone to go with you?"

"No," Mari shouted. "I mean, I won't be long. Tabasco can come with me."

"She'll be fine," Alex said as Mari started down the trail. "She just needs to pee, is all."

"Hurry back," David called after her, "and try not to get eaten by coyotes!"

Mari ran ahead into the woods, feeling like an idiot and half-hating her brothers. Why did they always insist on embarrassing her? A thirty-something-year-old woman shouldn't have to worry about the wrath of her little brothers.

Guided only by the light of her flashlight and the insistent barking of Tabasco just a few steps ahead of her, she searched for a secluded space amid the dead limbs and sandstone piles where she could have some privacy.

Mari was far enough away that she could just barely make out the murmur of her family and Rick around the fire pit. Above her she heard the lonely cry of a whippoorwill and what sounded like a barn owl, serenading the trail with their sad, solemn songs. Listening to them there in the stillness, Mari began to feel sad herself.

Her nervousness persisted, even after she was far enough away from the camp that she knew there was no chance of Rick accidentally stumbling across her as she knelt in the shrub. There was no knowing who else might be here. Occasionally she heard a rustle in the bushes and stood there frozen for a moment afraid someone was going to jump out at her. But then they went still again, and she continued on her way.

Calmed by the smell of mesquite smoke from a distant fire, she breathed a quick prayer as she waved her flashlight over a clump of cedars surrounded by long-necked beer bottles.

"Honestly," she said to herself with a shake of her head. "You wouldn't think it would be that hard to keep this place clean." As Tabasco ran circles around her, barking, she surveyed the damage with a feeling of deep irritation. A couple of cans of Corona, a fast food bag, the remains of a half-eaten hot dog bun, a bottle top—a human hand…

Mari stumbled back and let out a scream as she realized what she was seeing. There at the foot of a tree, half-submerged by the litter surrounding it, lay a dead body.

CHAPTER TWO

Mari stood there for several seconds struggling to get hold of herself. Stumbling across a dead body by accident was a lot to take in. With a heavy feeling, she forced herself to back away slowly. She rubbed her uneasy stomach.

Presently there came a loud patter of footsteps, and three figures burst into the clearing. A wave of relief washed over her as she realized it was her two brothers and Officer Rick.

"Mari, what's wrong?" Rick asked, shining his flashlight on her face. "Are you—"

But he broke off when he saw the body lying there. Alex nudged David and pointed to the bushes. No one spoke for a moment, and in the silence, Mari began to wish someone would say *something*.

"Nobody touches anything," Rick said as he began circling the area. "Alex, I left my phone at the campsite. Will you run and get it for me?"

Alex turned without a word and ran back in the other direction. Mari knew he would soon be telling their parents what she had discovered. She could almost hear them gasping in surprise, then muttering sadly as reality set in. *I'm telling you, that woman is cursed*, her father would say. *This is why she still isn't married.*

David came over and put his arm around Mari, who was still shaking. "Was he like this when you found him?"

"Of course he was," Mari replied, regaining her composure. "I have no idea how long he's been there."

"We would need a coroner to make an accurate estimate," Rick added. He knelt over the body shining a light on the victim's face. "But I think I have a pretty good idea *how* he died." He motioned to the torso, which was covered in gashes. "I think it's safe to assume someone was not happy with this guy."

"Is he carrying any ID?" Mari asked, who was already shifting into detective mode, perhaps as a way of coping with the shock. "We need to figure out who he is."

After a cursory examination of his pockets, Rick shook his head. "But everyone who comes here checks in with the ranger at the gate, so they might be able to give me a list of names."

To Mari's surprise, David spoke up. "That won't be necessary."

Rick turned the light to their faces, blinding Mari temporarily. "Why not?"

"Because I know who that is," David said. "It's Danny Soto. He opened up a taco truck right across the street from our burrito truck. And no, he was not very popular. Obviously, I hate seeing anyone die, but I can't say I'm particularly sad to see this one go."

Rick glared at David in annoyance. "Can I quote you on that?"

"I obviously didn't kill him," David stated, raising both hands. "But—and Alex will back me up on this—Danny was not a nice guy. It doesn't surprise me that he, apparently, made one too many enemies."

"You're going to have to be more specific," Rick said. There was a slight edge in his voice, which Mari thought was understandable given the circumstances.

20

"I mean, we had personally walked up to his taco truck and asked him not to set up shop right across from us," David said. "We even brought him a plate of our green chile pork tacos—one of the more expensive items on our menu. He took one look at the plate, picked it up, and chucked it out the window into the dirt."

"Okay, I get it," Rick responded. "The guy was a jerk."

"And we tried to explain to him how having two taco trucks in the same area would be bad for our business, without benefiting him in any real way. About halfway through the discussion he just started humming to himself as if we weren't even there. We tried to get his attention a couple of times, but he just kept humming. Eventually, we gave up and left." David shrugged.

"Really?" Mari said. "You just left?" She found it hard to believe that her brothers didn't retaliate. Although, Alex and David did have a way of wording stories to make themselves look like innocent victims.

"That's what I said," David repeated, looking down at him the body.

They stood there in silence for a moment reflecting on what had just happened. Wings flapped in the sky overhead, and moonlight trickled down through the branches. Mari shivered. She had half-hoped that getting out of town for the weekend would grant her a break from crime-solving, but in that effort, she had been disappointed.

Rick rose to his feet. "Where is your brother?" he asked impatiently. "He was supposed to have been back ten minutes ago."

"He and Mom and Dad probably got to talking," David answered. "They can't help it. We're a family of talkers."

"And you know, most of the time I don't mind," Rick continued. "But a man has just been killed, and we need the police out here immediately. I'll be right back." Mari watched with a sinking feeling as Rick ran from the clearing back in the direction of the campsite.

The moment he was gone, footsteps on the side trail to their left echoed through the night air, and Alex wandered back into the clearing.

"Are you kidding me?" David muttered.

"The police are on their way," Alex said reassuringly. "I called them a few minutes ago. Where's Rick?"

"What did you say exactly?" Mari asked, listening for the sound of Rick's returning footsteps.

"I told them you found a body in the woods. That's all." Alex shook his head. "I didn't confess murder or anything, okay. I'm not an idiot."

"I told them, Alex," David said. "I figured it would come out eventually."

"I see." Alex took a deep breath. "So it really is our friend Danny Soto. I was hoping it might be a look-a-like."

"Wait," Mari went on. "So you didn't mention to the police who it was that you found?"

"I mean, no," Alex replied, as though this should have been obvious. "It's dark, and it's at least conceivable that I wouldn't recognize the body. I figured it was better to distance ourselves from the crime as much as possible."

"We will see about that," Mari said with a hint of impatience. "Hopefully, that little tidbit isn't used against you."

Alex ignored her. "Did you already tell Rick we had been fighting?" he asked David.

"Yeah, but I didn't tell them about what happened last week."

Mari glanced from one brother to the other. "What happened last week?" she asked, her eyes glinting with suspicion in the half-darkness.

"There was an incident, I guess you could call it," David responded. "Danny came into the abandoned lot where we park our burrito truck and started handing out flyers promoting *his* taco truck. The man was completely shameless. So of course, Alex and I decided to scare him off."

"What did you do?" Mari asked. "Please, don't tell me you did something stupid."

"We didn't hurt the guy," David said.

"Just threatened to," Alex added. "And it worked. It was pretty impressive the way he backed off like David might actually burn his truck down."

Mari rubbed her forehead.

"What?" David threw his hands up. "We didn't do anything. Actions speak louder than words."

"The guy had it coming though," Alex chimed in, but David shushed him with a wave of his hand.

Tabasco sat at Mari's feet and began growling in agitation. At first, Mari had no idea what he was growling at, but then she saw it. A flashlight moved slowly down the trail toward them.

"Who could that possibly be?" David whispered as he, Alex, and Mari moved closer together. "Do you think someone is looking for him?"

"He must have been here with someone," Alex whispered. "What else would he have been doing in the middle of the woods?"

David nodded. "You mean like a friend?"

Soon the figure was close enough that they heard a woman's voice calling out faintly in the darkness. "Danny?" she cried. "Danny?"

As though with one mind, David and Alex ran forward to confront the woman before she discovered the body on her own. But they were too late. The woman stumbled on Danny's body all on her own, and as a result, let out a scream that could be heard throughout all of Tortoise Nation.

CHAPTER THREE

The screaming woman stepped into the light where Mari could see her. She was a slender young woman with pale skin, dark blue eyes, and dirty blonde hair tied back in a loose ponytail. She wore a green Tortoise Nation sweatshirt and yoga pants.

As Mari and her two brothers stepped closer, she glared back and forth at the three of them suspiciously. The way she looked at Danny's body, Mari guessed that the woman wondered if the three of them were to blame.

"We found him like this," Mari blurted out. "We already called the police."

"What...I..." The woman did her best to fight the tears.

"The police should be here any minute along with our friend Officer Rick Kinney," Mari continued. "They will figure out what happened to your friend."

"Who found him?" the woman asked, sniffling.

"I found him," Mari replied, coming forward and extending her hand. "My name is Marisol Ramirez, but you can call my Mari. How did you know him?"

The woman wiped away more tears, unable to take her eyes off the body. "I'm his girlfriend, Maeve Rivers. Or, I was. Danny and I were up at the Soto family lake house celebrating the anniversary of his business when Danny left."

"To venture into the woods in the middle of the night?" Mari asked. "Did he tell you where he was going?"

"We had a fire going in the stone hearth in the living room," Maeve explained. "Danny came out here to collect more wood. He has done the same thing loads of times in the past. It's not unusual. But when he didn't come back after half an hour, I began to worry. I came out here and—"

She broke off, forcing herself to look up at the moonlight.

Mari nodded sympathetically.

"Do you have any idea who might have wanted to kill Danny?" Mari asked cautiously. The sooner she figured out what happened to Danny Soto, the better. She knew that the town's detective wouldn't take kindly to her brothers if he found out that they had threatened the deceased.

"Not a clue," Maeve said with a shake of her head. "Danny didn't have any enemies that I know of."

Alex coughed, and Mari glared at him, hoping that he wouldn't interject with a snide comment.

"Please, continue," Mari encouraged her.

"The Sotos are a very wealthy family," Maeve went on. "Their lake house is one of the most expensive properties in the Hill Country. Danny was one of those people who was good at everything he touched. He even bought a taco truck last month and quickly turned it into a profitable business. His father's health has been failing for some time, and Danny was next in line to inherit the family business. Frankly, it baffles me that anyone would dream of hurting such a kind, talented man."

Both of Mari's brothers looked like they were eager to contradict her, but Mari shushed them with one of her looks.

"A taco truck?" Mari asked.

"To prove to his father that he could make money selling anything," Maeve responded. "Even a silly little taco. It was one of his proudest accomplishments. Danny was excited to prove to his father that he was a worthy Soto businessman."

"And he thought running a taco truck would do that?" Mari said, trying hard not to sound rude.

Maeve didn't seem to notice the skeptical tone in her voice. "He did, and also I think it was a way of proving to his father that he would be leaving the family business in good hands. I don't know how much longer Danny's father will be around. This might push him over the edge."

"I'm really sorry," Mari stated.

"I just can't believe it," Maeve said. "Danny was doing so well."

"The police will find who did this." Mari was beginning to regret that she hadn't brought a pen and notebook with her into the woods, but then again, she hadn't been expecting to stumble on a dead body. "There must be someone out there who has a grudge against him at least?"

Maeve froze, and a dark look flashed across her face for a second. It was an expression Mari had seen her father make when he realized that money was missing from the register. Finally, she shook her head.

"No," Maeve said stiffly. Mari was hardly convinced.

"So the two of you were dating," Mari went on. "How serious were you, if you don't mind me asking?"

"I expect we would have gotten engaged eventually," Maeve admitted. "We were already discussing moving in together."

"Here at the lake house?"

"No," Maeve answered. "Danny has a house in town. Although, has was talking about selling everything and moving to the lake house to live full-time."

By now the mesquite smell that filled the night air was beginning to dissipate and the sound of celebration that had been emanating from the lake for the last couple of hours subsided into an uneasy stillness. Mari offered to escort Maeve back to the campsite where she could meet Rick and undergo formal a questioning.

"I will stay with you if you'd like," Mari offered. "Or maybe I can call someone for you?" Maeve nodded.

"I had better call the family," Maeve said, clearing her throat. She started back toward the way she came.

"Are you sure you don't want to speak to the police?" Mari asked.

"I expect they will head to the lake house at some point tonight," Maeve replied, already reaching into her purse for her phone "I will gather the family." She turned around and walked back up the trail in the other direction.

"I feel sorry for her," Alex said when she had rounded the bend and disappeared.

"Yeah," Mari agreed. "But there is something she isn't telling us. Did you see her face when I asked her if anyone at all might have a grudge against Danny?"

"If you ask me, she's too trusting," David said. "She is lucky we aren't psychos."

"And she was obviously in love with Danny," Alex said in a disgruntled tone. "She was blinded to the fact that he was a pretty terrible person."

Tired of waiting, the three of them made the walk back to the campsite while Tabasco trotted ahead. When they arrived, they found Detective Price standing in front of the fire pit. His usual partner, Officer Penny, was nowhere to be seen. Tabasco was resting near the fire with a look of satisfaction on his face.

"That idiot dog ate the rest of the stew," Mr. Ramirez complained, glaring venomously at Tabasco. "I was looking forward to eating that!"

"Dad," Mari said with a sideways look at Detective Price and Rick. "I know you're hungry, but we have more pressing issues right now. A man has just been murdered."

"Big deal," her father muttered. "People die every day. But it's not every day that I get to eat your mother's Dutch oven stew."

Mari bit the side of her lip, grateful that not many officers seemed to have heard him. Her father was known for being insensitive when it came to serious topics like death.

"Why did you leave the body?" Rick asked. "Detective Price and I were just about to head over there."

"I heard voices," Detective Price chimed in.

"Don't forget the scream," Mr. Ramirez added.

"Oh, that was Maeve Rivers, the victim's girlfriend," Mari said apologetically. "I just spent the last few minutes talking to her."

"Well, where is she?" Rick scanned the campsite.

"At the Soto lake house," Mari answered. "She wanted to call Danny's family."

"Okay, well, Officer Penny is currently vacationing in the Bahamas, so it looks like I will be assisting the detective in this investigation." Rick paused for congratulations.

"This is a big deal, right?" Mari said. "Well then, good luck."

"Thanks." Rick smiled. "I mean it is awful that a man has been killed, but this is a big day for me. If all goes well, it could lead to a promotion. So if Maeve Rivers turns up again, or if the murderer wanders into the campsite and confesses everything, you know my number. Will you text me if anything happens?"

"Promise," Mari replied. She waved a small, sad goodbye as Rick gathered up his things and followed Detective Price.

CHAPTER FOUR

"Are we sure we want to stay here?" asked Mrs. Ramirez after the policemen had left. "In an hour or two, this place is going to be crawling with even more police and press."

"But we *just* finished setting up our tents," David argued. "I'm not about to take them all down and go home just because—"

He didn't finish the sentence, but he didn't have to. Mari knew that Alex and David weren't about to let Danny Soto ruin one more thing in their lives.

"I think David has a point," Mari said, kneeling down by the fire pit and gathering up the stew-encrusted plates. "This is nothing we haven't dealt with before." The Ramirez family had gotten remarkably good at continuing to work while the police and reporters swarmed the restaurant. "Besides, Rick has already gotten our statements, so they won't need to return here tonight. They might not even bother us at all."

Mr. Ramirez shook his head with a look of disdain. "There's going to be quite a bit of noise when the other campers find out a man was killed. The chatter alone is likely to keep us up all night."

"It's a weekend," Mari said as she tethered Tabasco to the front of her tent. "People would have been up all night shouting and partying anyway. Honestly, if you wanted to enjoy a quiet and relaxing weekend there are better ways of doing it."

Mr. Ramirez grimaced as if not wanting to be lectured about how to spend his time by his own daughter.

"We'll stay," he said. "But only because our money can't be refunded.

And, frankly, I'm too tired to make the drive home."

"I'll drive," Mrs. Ramirez added. "I would much rather be at home in my own bed, José. Next time just spring for the beach."

"So would I, believe me," said Mr. Ramirez. "But we're here, so we might as well get used to it. Anyway, we'll be home in a day or two."

With a collective groan, the family retired to their tents for the night. Despite her father's speculations, perfect silence reigned over the camp site broken only by the sounds of her parents arguing in the next tent. Mari lay there for about an hour listening to their heated whispers, not minding that they were keeping her up. As a teenager, they would have annoyed her, but by now she found their frequent arguments endearing rather than irritating.

"Besides," she whispered to herself, "it's not like they're going to be around forever." If there was one benefit to tonight, it was the sudden reminder that life was short.

Eventually, the light went off in the other tent, and her parent's voices fell silent. With a sigh of relief, Mari turned over thinking she might finally be able to sleep. But the sudden silence had the perverse effect of amplifying all other noises. Every time she heard the breaking of a twig or the rustle of branches, she worried that it might be the killer. The low hoot of an owl flying overhead in search of prey only heightened her anxiety.

She reached over and checked her phone. In a few hours dawn would break over the camp, and the air would be filled with the rustle of wildlife. But for now nothing stirred in the woods but a small animal—at least she hoped it was an animal—clambering over logs and fallen branches. If she had opened the tent and peered out, she felt sure that she might have seen the golden glowing eyes of a raccoon peering back at her.

But no, it couldn't have just been a raccoon. Lights flashed from behind a shrub. Mari stiffened, hardly daring to breathe. She heard the sound of footsteps on gravel and voices whispering to one another.

"Tortoises are huge," one of them said. "You've never seen a hundred-pound turtle. And they get to be really old, like centuries old. I read somewhere that there's a tortoise that's older than our country."

"Are you sure what you read wasn't fake?" said the other. "I mean, how would you even know how old a tortoise is?"

With a wave of relief, Mari realized it was her brothers. Climbing out of her sleeping bag, she slipped into her sneakers and out of the tent.

Tabasco trotted quietly alongside her as she scurried over logs, stones, and brambles in the direction of the voices. When she finally caught up with them, they were so engaged in their argument that they didn't hear the patter of her feet as she snuck up behind them.

"All I'm saying is," Alex continued, "the average man on the street doesn't know the difference between a turtle and a tortoise."

"Well, maybe it's time someone *tortoise*," David said with a broad smile. Alex groaned loudly.

"Where do you get those terrible jokes?" Mari said. Alex and David both flinched and turned around in unison, their faces deathly pale. "You know, you really should be quieter."

"Oh, it's you," David responded, "You really ought to know better than to go sneaking up on people in the middle of the night. I thought you were a raving lunatic."

"That's debatable," Alex muttered. "I mean, there's no telling what I might do if I thought someone was about to attack me. Remember when we were kids and you hid in the pantry all those hours just to get me back for *borrowing* money from your wallet? You're lucky I didn't knife you."

"Oh, I remember," Mari said. "And you didn't borrow that money. You stole it. You see, borrowing means that you eventually pay the person back."

"Well, I had already spent it," Alex added.

"Mari, what are you doing here?" David changed the subject.

"Wondering the same thing about you," Mari replied.

"We both got a text from Kacee Baker informing us that there was going to be a house party at one of the fancy places by the lake. It's been a while since I've been to a good kegger."

"Do you think that's wise given what happened tonight?" Mari asked.

"Sure," Alex commented. "Danny Soto dies, and now we can't have fun?"

"Besides, it's not like there won't be a few buzzkills keeping people in line," David went on. "You're coming now, aren't you?"

"I'm not a buzzkill," Mari stated in a defiant voice.

"Sure you're not," he sarcastically replied.

Mari rolled her eyes and followed her brothers as they walked through the woods.

As much as Mari wanted to argue with this, she knew they had a point. She wasn't about to let them venture off on their own, not when a killer could be lurking at every turn. Of course, there was also the reality that it had been around ten years since she had attended a wild party, and she wondered if she would enjoy it as much as she had back in college.

"Do you even know how to socialize like a normal person?" Alex asked, shoving aside the last limb in their path to reveal a lake dazzled by moonlight. A row of large wood-frame houses stood on the other side of it. Mari saw their destination in the distance, an enormous manor lit up like a birthday cake and teeming with dozens of small figures.

"Yes, I know how to party like a normal person," Mari stated. "My life isn't all Mexican food. I did have a life once, remember?"

But even she sounded unsure as they made their way toward the lofty front porch. A pair of speakers at least as tall as her father was blasting music, causing the walls to rattle and vibrate. A couple of party-goers grilled steaks and sausages while a young woman stood holding the stub of a cigarette, drunkenly cheering on a friend who was batting at several blue and silver balloons like a cat.

Mari had seen enough mysteries where the victim was accidentally murdered by a couple of careless partyers to be on her guard for clues. When a girl wearing only a lace bra and a pair of short shorts offered her a glass filled with champagne, she refused. Besides, she reminded herself, her brothers would probably be passed out by the end of the night, and it would be her responsibility to take them home.

Mari was on her way into the living room when she noticed a golden plaque hanging on the wall. Intrigued, she broke away from David who was happily chatting with the girl in the lace bra and strode toward it. Her eyes darted to a familiar name. *Soto*.

Mari let out a low whistle as she realized, for the first time, where she was. Alex and David had unknowingly led her straight to Danny Soto's lake house.

CHAPTER FIVE

Mari entered the Soto's lake house, leaving David behind on the patio. Alex had already gone inside and disappeared into a crowd of people. There was little chance of her finding him again. Mari held tight to Tabasco and began looking around.

Entering the wood-paneled living room, she was surprised to find a display case full of brass instruments. At the edge of the room where the crowd had thinned a little, clusters of people stood together holding red cups and long-necked beer bottles and attempting to talk over the noise and music. Others sat alone on the plush carpet, their backs against the wall, looking thoughtful.

Not really the best place to question people, Mari thought with a sigh of dissatisfaction as she stepped over a mound of trash. If anyone here knew Danny was dead, they gave no indication of it.

A brief investigation of the kitchen revealed a bearded man with several tattoos helping himself to a slice of chocolate cake. He glared at Mari as she walked past him and went on eating the cake with his fingers. A cocktail bar had been set up on the counter stacked with bottles and mixers, many of them already empty. Below it on the floor stood a blue and white cooler loaded with sodas.

Not wanting to drink, but also not wanting to look out of place, Mari grabbed a soda and, because it was quite cold, wrapped it in a paper towel. Then, searching the counter until she found the last of the red cups, she poured the drink inside and hoped it would help her blend in.

Feeling sure now that no one would notice or care if she took a look around the place, Mari wandered through the rooms and hallways of the lake house getting a feel for the layout and the locations of the various guests.

Through a window in the back of the house, Mari saw the second patio. At first, she confusedly thought it was the same patio through which she had come into the house. But that patio had faced the lake, and this one brushed up against the edge of the woods. A few guys had gathered recliners and lounge chairs from inside the house and had arranged them in a circle around a bonfire. They took turns tossing pieces of trash into the fire. A young woman wearing a black beanie played guitar and sang. A couple of guys in beer-stained polo shirts took out their phones and began waving them in the air, in a gesture that started out ironic and slowly became sincere.

"Was I really like this once?" Mari said to her dog Tabasco. "How does anyone have the energy for this? I guess I must be turning into my Abuela. I would so much rather be at home in my own bed."

Mari was still trying to figure out when she had grown old as she climbed the stairs to the second level of the house and found a new set of rooms on either side of the hallway. She knew she was treading on dangerous territory. While the rooms on the lower level had all been guest rooms, this had the look of an area that was closed off to visitors. As far as she could tell there was no one around except for a girl in a baseball cap and hoodie lying in the hall, fast asleep.

Mari brushed past the sleeping woman and began examining the rooms, one by one.

There was nothing of note in the first three rooms she entered, but the fourth proved to be the bedroom of Danny Soto. A trophy display case lined the wall showing off his various achievements. Mari's eyes were drawn to a wall full of pictures hanging just over the display case showing Danny and several dozen other boys. Mari suspected that he had belonged to a fraternity while in school.

An unmade bed was against the opposite wall. A woman's blue jacket lay draped on top of it. On the wall above the bed were additional framed pictures. In several of them, he stood alongside a petite blonde woman who Mari at first mistook for Maeve before realizing it must have been his own mother, to whom she bore a striking resemblance. It was hard to say they looked happy. His expression was perpetually tense and uncertain while a sense of unease lurked in her eyes and the rigid lines of her face.

Most curious of all, in the center of this last set of pictures hung a framed diploma, except that the frame had no diploma in it. It contained only the generic picture – a black and white photograph of a couple of teens laughing on an idyllic university campus - that came with every frame. Mari's concentration was broken when Tabasco let out a low growl.

"It's sad, isn't it?" came a voice from behind her. "Mom always hoped one day he would get his act together and graduate. So far he's done nothing but disappoint her."

Mari flinched and turned around. There in the doorway stood a young man who might have been a younger version of the one in the pictures, except that he had a more pinched appearance and his brown hair hung loosely all the way down to his shoulders. "You must be—"

"Leo," said the young man, taking off his leather jacket and tossing it on the bed next to the blue one. "Leo Soto. I don't blame you for coming in here. Girls are always showing up in his room."

"It's nothing like that," Mari replied. "It's not what you think at all."

"Well, I wouldn't blame you if you were," Leo continued. "He has that sort of power over women. They just throw themselves at him. Sometimes literally."

"I guess he didn't put up much of a struggle," Mari said.

"No," Leo responded with a sad shake of his head. "He never does."

There was something about the way he spoke this last sentence that troubled her. "Do you ... I mean, do you know where Danny is right now?" she asked.

Leo shook his head. "Probably out with his girl of the week. It's sad because he could have been so much more than what he is. Growing up he was always the special one - the one who would run the family business. He is so coddled by Mom and Dad that he never put in a real day's work until he bought himself a silly little food truck. But that was just a rouse to stop Dad from cutting him out of the will. My parents always threaten that, but I doubt they would ever actually do it."

"Danny has a girlfriend, right?" Mari stated. "I've met her. They seemed pretty serious. Even discussing marriage from what she told me."

Leo didn't look at all surprised. "Yeah, well, that's never stopped him from getting with the ladies before," he said.

"Look, Leo, I don't know how to tell you this ..." Mari began, but her speech was cut short by a noise of insistent pounding from downstairs. Tabasco barked.

Leo snatched his coat from the bed and ran to the door. "Crap, we'd better get out of here," he said with an urgent look on his face. "That was the warning signal."

"Signal for what?" Mari asked.

"Either my parents are here, or the cops. Or both. Either way, I'm in a lot of trouble." Leo threw on his coat and in a split-second, he was gone.

CHAPTER SIX

Grabbing Tabasco by the leash, Mari led him through the hallway and down the stairs into the living room. So much was happening all at once that she was having trouble making sense of it. Why had no one told Leo that his brother was dead? Did his parents even know? Had Maeve known Danny was cheating on her? And why was Maeve nowhere to be found?

By the time she reached the main level an ominous quiet had fallen over the house. The music had stopped, and the majority of party-goers had already left.

Leo stood in the center of the living room. His parents had just come in through the sliding-glass door and had paused in their tracks when they saw him. A tense face-off ensued in which neither party seemed willing to move, and the rest of the partygoers watched nervously from the sidelines. The bearded man with tattoos stood at the kitchen counter with a half-eaten chicken wing in one hand. He looked anxiously from Leo to Leo's parents as if trying to assess if the party would be allowed to continue.

"Is this what you get up to when we leave the house?" Mrs. Soto finally asked. She wore a light pink coat and diamond studs on her ears. "We haven't even been gone for three hours."

Mari heard the anger in her voice, but, more than that, a sense of despair and disappointment. She wondered if the Sotos now viewed both of their sons as failures.

"All I wanted," Leo said, adopting a more belligerent tone than he had used upstairs, "was one night of fun. I don't think that's too much to ask. I've been working like a dog, and I don't even get one night to do what I want with my friends?"

"You should have told us how you felt," Mr. Soto replied, a frail-looking man with a pale face and thinning gray hair. "If I had known you wanted to throw a party with a few hundred of your closest friends …"

"Cut it out, Dad," Leo said heatedly. "How come I have to be responsible every night of the year, and Danny gets to do whatever he wants?" Mr. Soto opened his mouth to speak, but Leo cut him off. "Danny can insult you to your face, and you won't lift a finger because he's the golden boy. He's even going to inherit the company although he never bothered to graduate from college. I graduated, Dad. What about me, huh?"

"Leo," Mr. Soto said in a quiet voice, "your brother is dead."

Leo scoffed like it was a joke. "Don't even try that with me," he said. "It's not funny."

"No, it's not," Mrs. Soto added. "It's not funny at all. No one is joking here."

If Mari had thought the party was dismal before, that was nothing to the despair that settled over it in the wake of this announcement. The bearded man in the kitchen dropped his chicken wing with a guilt-stricken look on his face. In the distance, someone began crying.

"Great," Leo muttered, shooting a venomous look at his parents as if it was somehow their fault that Danny had died. "He's not even alive anymore, and he's still ruining my night."

Before they could respond, Leo turned around and left the room.

The moment he left, the Sotos found themselves hounded with questions. Was Danny really dead? Where was his body? Who had found him? Where was Maeve? Was she okay? How did he die?

As Mari surveyed the outpouring of grief, a horrible feeling welled up in the pit of her stomach. She was beginning to wonder if David and Alex had been alone in their hatred of Danny. Danny had dozens of mourners, maybe hundreds. It was only a matter of time before her brothers became the principal suspects in his murder.

She wanted to warn them, but they were nowhere to be found. It was a huge house, and it might take her all night to find them. Maybe as the news of Danny's death made its way throughout the house, they would be drawn back out into the main room.

"Listen," Mr. Soto shouted, addressing the crowd. "All I can tell you right now is that Danny was found dead in the woods tonight. The police are actively investigating what happened as we speak. Now, please leave us in peace."

Before Mari could leave to look for her brothers, Detective Price entered the room. Outside on the patio, she saw Officer Rick Kinney interviewing a handful of partygoers. Mari's heart pounded.

Mari tried her best to avoid Detective Price and Rick. She resorted to escaping into the kitchen and pretending to look through the contents of the fridge. It seemed like an okay plan until the detective and his new partner were no longer blocking the exits.

"I'm sorry to say the party is over," Detective Price told the crowd. "I'm also sorry to say that I need all of you to stick around for at least the next hour because Officer Kinney and I need everybody's name and whereabouts this evening. No one leaves without our permission."

There was a collective groan, and Mari cleared her throat, trying to hide Tabasco with the fridge door. One look at her bulldog and she would be subjected to more interviews. Though the chances of her leaving without being seen were growing slim.

As if hoping to hasten that unavoidable moment, Tabasco broke away and trotted out of the kitchen into the living room, his tongue lolling happily. Mari snapped her fingers and tried to catch him before he grabbed the attention of the police, but she was too late.

"Hey, fella," Rick said, one brow raised in suspicion, as he knelt down and examined his collar. "How did you get in here?"

He threw a puzzled glance at Detective Price. Just then Mari came walking out of the kitchen, her hands in her back pockets, blushing furiously.

"Hi," she said. "What a coincidence, huh?"

She wanted to melt into the floor, but Rick didn't seem angry or alarmed. "What are you doing here, Mari?" he asked.

"Probably the same thing she's always doing," Detective Price said out of the corner of his mouth. "Investigating."

"Maybe *I* should be your new partner, detective," Mari said casually. When no one laughed, she added, "Joke... it was a joke."

"I said no one could leave until we had finished getting statements,"

Detective Price responded, "but in your case, I'll make an exception. You go home, Mari. Wherever home is for you tonight. I know where to find you. Officer Kinney and I have our hands full at the moment."

"You mean you're not going to question me at all?" Mari asked, feeling both relieved and slightly disappointed.

"No at this exact moment," he said. "Keep your phone on. I'll be coming by to talk to you tomorrow."

Mari smiled awkwardly at Rick, who nodded curtly and escorted her out the door onto the patio.

"Well," she said as she turned to face him, her eyes downcast, "I guess this is where I leave you."

"Not yet," Rick said. "I'm not going to let you walk all the way back to camp yourself, not when there's a killer on the loose."

Mari wanted to protest that she could take care of herself, but she appreciated the gesture. "What about David and Alex?"

Rick raised his brows in surprise.

"Are they here?" he asked. "Strange. I haven't seen them anywhere."

CHAPTER SEVEN

Mari returned to the camp site and stayed up half the night puzzling over the events of the last several hours. Alone in her tent, she waited for the stir of her brother's feet shattering the night's stillness, but they still hadn't returned by the time she began nodding off to sleep. Tabasco guarded the door to her tent. Mari figured that he would alert her when her brothers finally got back.

"Something strange is going on," she said to Tabasco, who yawned grumpily. "Do you think Alex and David are in trouble?"

Mari had a terrible feeling she was going to wake up the next morning to find that her brothers had been arrested. They hadn't been helping themselves the way they had been talking about Danny. He might have been a jerk, but it seemed that he had as many friends as he had enemies. Word of Danny's run in with the Ramirez boys would eventually get out.

Mari's parents slept soundly in the next tent. They had fallen asleep before David and Alex slipped out for the night. They had no idea of the troubles they might be facing when they woke up—that both of their sons might be branded as criminals. They hadn't done it of course, but right now there was evidence that pointed to them. And in a town like Mari's, that was as good as a conviction.

***

By the time Mari awoke the next morning, David and Alex had returned to the campsite. Her mother and father were quietly cooking a breakfast of bacon, eggs, and canned beans. If either of them noticed that their two sons had been gone for most of the night, they didn't mention it.

"After breakfast, I think I'm going to go back to the crime scene," Mari said, emerging from her tent in a knitted pullover and a pair of sweatpants. The air was damp and chilly, and a light mist lay over the campground.

"Why?" asked Mr. Ramirez, glaring at Tabasco who was eyeing the bacon with a covetous gaze. "You were out there for over an hour last night."

"There are a lot of things you can't see in the dark," Mari responded, grabbing the plates from her gym bag and beginning to lay them out around the fire pit. "I want to go back to the trail and make sure I didn't miss anything."

"I don't see why you can't just let the police do their job," Mrs. Ramirez argued.

"Sometimes the police miss things," Mari continued. Of course, there was more to it than that. She had an uncomfortable feeling the police had already made up their minds about David and Alex. If so, they might be quick to dismiss evidence that contradicted the story they were building.

"Well, if you must go, take your brothers with you," Mrs. Ramirez replied. "Heaven knows I don't need you getting murdered while trying to catch a murderer."

"I'm in," Alex muttered, inhaling a few slices of bacon. "This part of the campsite is a total bore anyway."

"True dat," David added. "I could use the walk."

"They say fresh air does wonders for a hangover," Mari commented quietly. Alex and David both glared at her.

David held a slice of bacon in the air above Tabasco, who stood on his hind legs to reach it.

"Give me that," said Mr. Ramirez, snatching it out of his hand with frustration. "The amount I pay for this food, I'm not about to watch it disappear down a dog's gullet."

"Chill out, Pops," Alex replied. "Watch this. He still thinks I have the bacon. This dog is hilarious." He held his fist over Tabasco's head. The dog whined greedily and stumbled toward him with a curious look.

Alex laughed and rubbed Tabasco's ears playfully. "It's like he thinks hands spontaneously generate food." Tabasco scowled at him in disappointment.

After breakfast, the three siblings ventured back out into the woods with Tabasco in tow. A light fog rose over the foliage and fallen oaks on either side of the trail, and a gray light slanted through the canopy above with no hint of blue skies behind it.

"So what happened after I left last night?" Mari asked as they approached the bend in the path where the murder had taken place.

"That depends on when you left," David replied. "Alex and I found a group playing video games. That's what we did most of the night. Then the police showed up."

"Yeah, did you know that was Danny's place we went to last night?" Alex added. "What are the odds of that? I had no idea until the police broke up the party. Some guys jumped out the window because they were freaked out that Danny was dead."

"Sounds like fun." Mari took a deep breath. "Did you tell anyone you knew Danny or that you found his body?"

"Why would I do that?" Alex narrowed his eyes. "I'm not that brainless, despite what you might think."

"I don't think I've ever been in a room where so many people were panicking," David went on. "I think they were all afraid of getting arrested or being haunted by Danny's ghost for partying in his house without him."

"Did the police question you?" Mari asked, though she already suspected she knew the answer.

"For like an hour," Alex answered. "Detective Price grilled us like crazy. It's like he doesn't trust us or something. But we told him we didn't do anything."

"I don't think they talked to anyone else for as long as they talked to us," David pointed out. "That's why we got back so late. Or I guess so *early*."

"Wait," Alex interjected. "They did keep Danny's little brother around for a while. Man, it must suck being related to that guy."

"I know what you mean, bro." David nodded.

Mari said nothing. Instead, she examined the foliage leading up to the spot where they had found Danny's body. In the gray light of morning, she saw broken limbs and places where the grass had obviously been trampled. It looked like Danny had been running through the undergrowth before he died.

Alex looked at her expectantly. "You wouldn't happen to know if we *are* prime suspects, would you? Because the number of questions that detective asked me has me a little worried."

Mari knew that feeling all too well, having been on the receiving end of several of Detective Price's interrogations. "It is possible. We found the body and then we turned up at the Soto family lake house. And then there's your little argument you had about his taco truck. What did the detective ask you?"

"He asked us where we were all night like a million times," Alex answered.

A prickly feeling of discomfort crept over Mari as she realized she hadn't heard from Rick for several hours. Were the police preparing a case against her family? Gazing bleakly into the bushes, she thought she might be sick. A circle was being drawn around her brothers, and the circle was tightening.

What a way to spend a holiday.

CHAPTER EIGHT

When they returned to the campsite half an hour later, Mari was surprised to find her parents packing up their things. Mrs. Ramirez was folding the tents while Mr. Ramirez poured a kettle full of water onto the fire pit.

"Are we leaving already?" Mari asked. "What's going on?"

"Your father has decided he can't spend another day out here," said Mrs. Ramirez in an annoyed tone. "He wants to go home to the restaurant."

"That's not what I said," Mr. Ramirez intervened. He hurriedly stuffed pots and dishes back into his wife's brown canvas bag. "I just think it would be good for us. It would help us get our minds off the murder and the police investigation. If we leave now, we can be open in time for the lunch."

"It would help *you*," Mrs. Ramirez reiterated as she folded a beach towel. "You haven't taken more than half a day off of work since we got married almost forty years ago. Are you married to me or the restaurant? Sometimes I have no clue."

"That restaurant is our livelihood, Paula," Mr. Ramirez responded. "I don't care if we win a cruise to the Bahamas. I won't do anything that will put the restaurant in jeopardy. And we had our fun hanging around the campfire for one night. Our regulars will thank us for coming back early."

Mari sighed. Her parents had been having this argument for as long as she could remember, and it was unlikely they were going to reach some sort of compromise. Her mother was always upset that her father never spent the money to take her somewhere nice. Her father just hated to spend money. He was the ultimate penny pincher.

"You do realize that you argue about this every summer," she said, grabbing a granola bar from her backpack.

"I know," Mr. Ramirez replied. "But your mother knows what the restaurant means to me. Besides, coming to Tortoise Nation hasn't done us any favors."

"I should have stayed home with Abuela," Mrs. Ramirez muttered. "The house is empty. The restaurant is closed for the weekend. She is the one having the real vacation right now."

***

Mari's father dropped her off at her apartment on the east side of town, where she fed Tabasco and changed into her work clothes. It didn't seem right that she should have to work when she was supposed to have the weekend off. But, of course, she wouldn't have gotten much rest camping in Tortoise Nation anyway.

"Focus, Mari," she told herself as she drove through the sleepy gray streets of the city on her way to Lito Bueno's Mexican Restaurant. Her dad could always tell when her mind was on something other than waiting tables. But right now she had no interest in working. What she felt instead was an urgency to find the true killer and exonerate her brothers before they could be taken in.

She thought it was strange how, when she was in the thick of investigating a murder, she did things she would never normally do. The flow of adrenaline made her downright determined. The knowledge that the killer was somewhere nearby plotting didn't scare her. Instead, it filled her with a reckless sort of pride. She had helped people escape sticky fates before. Her brothers were no different. And they were family. Not to mention that the family business might tank if the Ramirez boys were suddenly branded as cold blooded killers. The Sotos wouldn't rest until her father's Mexican restaurant went bankrupt.

Mari arrived at her family's restaurant to find her family and a small crew of staff crew getting ready to open. Mrs. Ramirez warmed up the oven while David and Alex rummaged through the kitchen looking for taco ingredients. Abuela had even come in to start on the homemade tortillas.

"What a way to spend a vacation," David said.

"At least now we can sell tacos and burritos in peace," Alex said in a jovial tone. "I say we make a *Taco Danny* special and sell it to his grieving fan club."

"Alex," Mari snapped. "That's exactly the kind of talk that will get you into trouble."

David and Alex paused and stared at her as if she were speaking a foreign language.

"Sorry," Alex weakly apologized. "I didn't realize we were running all of our management decisions past you now."

"It isn't funny," Mari said. She placed her hands on her hips to stop herself from waving them in Alex's face. "The police are on the hunt for a killer, and you two are at the top of their list. So if I were you, I'd keep my mouth shut and maybe try to seem a *little* sorry that Danny is dead."

Mari had gotten so caught up in her speech that she hadn't heard Chrissy, the waitress, unlocking the front door. So it came as a shock when she led Officer Rick Kinney into the room a moment later.

"Hi, y'all," Rick said, taking off his jacket. "Am I interrupting something?"

"No, you aren't," Mari responded, though her cheeks burned crimson. "I guess you're here to interview me?"

"I am," Rick answered in an apologetic tone, as though to suggest he didn't particularly want to do it. "Detective Price asked me to drop by and bring you into the station for questioning."

"Fine," Mari said as she grabbed her keys and purse. "I could use a break from my *break* anyway."

"And I could use some lunch," Rick replied. Mari rolled her eyes, unsure if she could stand being around her brothers for much longer.

"You're right," Mari agreed. "Lunch sounds good. But I don't want to eat here. I'm supposed to have today off. Let's go somewhere else."

"Where?" Rick raised his eyebrows.

"How about somewhere I never get to go." Mari looked out the window at the restaurant across the street.

***

The Lucky Noodle stood across the street from Lito Bueno's Mexican Restaurant and was, as its owner never tired of pointing out, the only traditional Chinese restaurant in town. Mr. Chun was about the same age as Mr. Ramirez and had been managing his business for about as long. The two men had been at each other's throats since Mari was in diapers. Recently they had each filed restraining orders to prevent the other from coming into their restaurant.

But Mari was allowed.

Mr. Ramirez had used countless meaningless threats to prevent his own children from eating at the Lucky Noodle. So, of course, they had visited whenever they thought they could get away with it because it annoyed José Ramirez more than anything. At one point Alex had even dated Mr. Chun's daughter, Jia, who co-managed the restaurant.

"I used to be so afraid of coming here," Mari said as they walked through the door and the smell of sautéed vegetables wafted toward them. "I thought Dad was going to jump out from behind a potted plant in the dining room and yell at me. But whenever I walked past, I couldn't get over how good the smells were. Eventually, I made up my mind I had to try it."

"And you liked it?" Rick asked, who seemed to have forgotten for a moment that he was supposed to be conducting a police interview.

"It's a nice change from rice and beans," Mari said. "Sometimes I get so tired of our menu."

"I grew up eating here," Rick replied. "We used to eat here every Sunday right after church. Mom isn't much of a cook."

"Really? *Your* mom?" Mari smiled. "I never would have guessed."

Mari went through the buffet line and piled her plate high with steamed broccoli, sautéed mushrooms, orange chicken, and egg fried rice. Rick got a small plate of noodles and sat staring at it for some time.

"Oh, my," Mari commented in a casual tone. "Suddenly you aren't very chatty. Are you going to arrest my brothers?"

Rick paused for a moment before responding.

"I know you've been dying to ask me that," he answered, scratching the side of his chin. "I'm sorry, Mari. Your brothers are under investigation. At the moment, they are our biggest leads."

"Why is that?"

Rick studied her face as if trying to word his answer very carefully. "Okay, I will tell you. But just know that I am doing everything in my power to figure out what really happened."

"Now, you have to tell me, Rick," Mari said, dousing her rice with soy sauce. "Besides, my brothers know they're in deep water."

"Well, neither of them have a good alibi for the time of the murder. Of course, they were with you when the body was found, but our examination of the wounds suggests that Danny was killed hours before you found him. Do you know where your brothers were late yesterday afternoon?"

Mari shook her head. "No. But they are not murderers. They can hardly make their beds in the morning."

"I know they aren't," Rick responded. He took a deep breath. "I'm working on proving that they weren't in Tortoise Nation at the time of the murder."

"Is that it?" Mari asked, glancing around the restaurant. She spotted Jia Chun, at the front counter.

"I wish," Rick said quietly. "Detective Price knows about the threats. Did you know that your brothers broke into Danny Soto's food truck?"

"What?" Mari shook her head. "No. I knew about the threats and the arguing, but they neglected to tell me that little detail. I can't believe this."

"Now you see why the detective's investigation is centered on them at the moment," Rick continued, dipping an egg roll into his sweet and sour sauce. "He can't deny the facts. Danny Soto opened a taco truck right across the street from them, and in a matter of weeks Danny is threatened, and his truck is broken into."

"I understand," Mari agreed. "But I stand by my brothers. They are not responsible for Danny's murder."

"Danny is proving to be the golden boy we keep hearing about," Rick went on. "Apparently, his father had high hopes for him opening up his own food truck and making it successful. He had a bright future ahead of him. A family business to inherit. His father's fortune."

This was all very interesting, and it gave Mari a clearer picture of the inner workings of Danny's family, as well as providing a context for the fight she had witnessed the night before involving Danny's brother Leo. She had been so absorbed in Rick's story that she didn't realize she had been picking at her vegetables.

"Sorry, I couldn't help overhearing." Jia Chun approached the table glancing down at the way Mari had been sloppily holding her chopsticks. "Danny Soto was an old friend of mine. In fact, he was in here just a few weeks ago."

"And you talked to him?" Mari asked. She hoped that Jia's intentions weren't sour. After all, she had dated one of Mari's brothers in the past and it did not end well.

"He was pretty depressed," Jia said. "He told me about his fight with Alex and David. He didn't think it was fair that the Ramirez family had a monopoly on Mexican food in this town. That's why he decided on tacos. But apparently, your brothers couldn't handle it, Mari."

"And here we go," Mari muttered. She clenched her jaw as Jia let her true intentions shine like sweat on Mr. Chun's forehead.

"Also, everyone knows about the food fight," Jia added. "Maturity means nothing to those idiots."

"Food fight?" Mari blurted out. "Really, Jia?"

Jia nodded. "Yeah. Danny said it was the messiest thing he had ever witnessed. Your brothers threw food at him, and it took all day for him to hose down the taco truck. All Ramirez men are absolute pigs."

"That didn't stop you from dating one," Mari pointed out.

"You bring that up again, Mari, and I will—"

"Okay," Rick shouted, holding up his hands. "The two of you need to stop it."

"You're lucky no one was hurt," Jia commented.

"Only someone like you would find herself *injured* from a piece of flying lettuce." Mari couldn't help herself. "Thank heavens there were no beans involved."

"Well." Rick cleared his throat and stood up to leave. "I can see why you hardly ever come here, Mari."

CHAPTER NINE

An hour later, Mari was seated outside Detective Price's office waiting for him to invite her in for questioning. She tugged nervously at the collar of her shirt. A cold rain was falling in the streets, but in the police station, it was uncomfortably warm.

Her conversation with Rick and Jia over lunch had not left her optimistic about the fate of her brothers. She felt even less reassured when she walked out of the Lucky Noodle and saw a line of people jostling to get into Lito Bueno's Mexican Restaurant before the rain started falling. One of her brothers had posted a sign at the front of the restaurant advertising their *Taco Danny* special.

"That sign," Mari said, shaking her head grimly. "They joked about a *Taco Danny* special, but I didn't think they would actually do it."

"Yeah." Rick shrugged, unsure what to say.

"They could have at least saved it for the food truck," Mari mentioned. "Less of an audience."

"They probably changed their minds when they saw the weather," Rick replied. "I don't know many people who gather around food trucks in the rain, do you?"

Even with all the warnings she had given them, it was hard to believe how foolish her brothers were behaving. They were like two little school boys, dancing on the Principal's last nerves. Mari thought it ridiculous that she had to remind herself that her brothers weren't teenagers anymore. They sure acted like it.

Mari sat alone with her thoughts after Rick returned to his desk. A cool breeze blasted through the room as the front doors opened. An older man and woman entered the building together. The man wore a suit, and the woman had on a light tan trench coat. They stuck close to each other with the nervous air of two people who had never been in a police station before. Somehow it reminded Mari of Dorothy and the Scarecrow in *The Wizard of Oz*.

Rick left his desk to address them. "Can I help you?" he asked.

"We would like to file a missing person's report," the man said. "This is what you do when a person goes missing, right?"

"And who, may I ask, is missing?" Rick grabbed a piece of paper.

"Our daughter," the man replied. "Her name is Maeve Rivers."

Rick paused and glanced up at the faces of the couple. He looked across the room at Mari. Mari gulped and sat up straighter as she listened.

"How long has she been missing?" Rick asked.

"We haven't heard from her since yesterday," the man said. "Sometime around three or four in the afternoon is when she left the house. She told us she was on her way to Tortoise Nation to meet Danny Soto, her boyfriend. We didn't think anything of it. They've been serious for a while now. Gladys waited up for her but she never came home, and she isn't answering her phone. We are very worried, Officer. We don't know what else to do."

Rick continued writing. "And what does your daughter look like?"

"Blonde, very blonde hair," her mother Gladys answered. "Petite and slender. She has a tattoo of a star on her left ankle."

"Can you remember what she was wearing the last time you saw her?" Rick continued.

Gladys hesitated. "I actually don't remember. I wasn't paying much attention. She usually dresses casual. Oh, she has this blue jacket that she wears pretty often."

"Okay," Rick replied. "Do you happen to have any pictures?"

"Why yes, of course," Gladys responded. She dug through her purse until she found a small photo. She handed it to Rick, who looked it over and clipped it to his report. Mari regretted that she wasn't close enough to see it herself.

"Look, Mr. and Mrs. Rivers, normally we don't take action until a person has been missing at least forty-eight hours, but I will present your report to my boss." Rick nodded.

At that moment the door to Detective Price's office opened, and Leo Soto came walking out. He looked huffy and made no eye contact with anyone in the room as he stormed out of the building into the rainy street.

"Next, please," came the voice of Detective Price. "Mari Ramirez, I think that would be you."

Mari rose and went into his office, wishing she could have stayed in the lobby a few minutes longer to hear the rest of Rick's interview with the Rivers family. While the detective rifled through his filing cabinet, she contemplated pulling out her phone and texting Rick what she was thinking, but she decided against it. She needed to tell him about the blue jacket she had seen on Danny Soto's bed the night before. Maeve had to have gone back to the house at some point that night. Something must have happened to her.

Unable to help herself, Mari reached into her purse and pulled out her phone. She had a voice mail, but she would check it later. She texted Rick, *Y'all need to search the lake house. I saw Maeve's jacket there.*

A minute later, she received a reply. *We searched the place last night. Nothing.*

"Miss Ramirez," Detective Price finally said, shutting the filing cabinet with a loud bang. Mari hurried to put her phone away. "I understand that you, once again, discovered the victim's body."

"I did," Mari replied. She recounted the story of how she had gone into the woods to relieve herself and how she had stumbled across the body in the process. He listened with great interest as she recalled the events of the next several hours including the arrival of Rick and her brothers and their panicked encounter with Maeve Rivers.

"You know, we're still looking for her," Detective Price said. "At this moment she's possibly our most critical witness."

The detective asked a few questions about Maeve. Finally, he returned to the topic that she had discussed with Rick at the Lucky Noodle—the involvement of Mari's brothers.

"By all accounts, their behavior toward the victim was rather abusive," the detective said. "The only two people in denial about this are Alex and David themselves."

"I understand," Mari said. "I know the cards have been stacked against them and I'm not making excuses for what they did. But they aren't killers, detective."

"What did they do exactly?" he asked, narrowing his eyes.

"Is this some type of tactic to get me to confess something?" Mari asked. "Because I think you already know what I am referring to."

Detective Price stood up. "Do you know where your brothers were yesterday afternoon before reaching the camp site?"

Mari drew a deep breath. "They were getting ready for the trip I suppose. They were probably grabbing a bite to eat or filling their car with gas. Normal stuff."

"So you don't know where they were," the detective continued, raising his eyebrows.

Mari shook her head. There was no good way of answering that question because the truth was that she didn't know.

CHAPTER TEN

As Mari was leaving the station, she remembered the missed call and lingering voicemail on her cell phone. It was David. Mari held the phone to ear and eagerly listened to what her brother had to say.

Mari, you'd better get over here quick. Mom and Dad are having another one of their arguments. It's loud enough for customers to hear, and we have a packed house. Alex already explained to the lunch crowd that they're just rehearsing for a play, but I don't think they buy it. You're the only person who can calm them down when they get worked up like this. Come to the restaurant.

Click.

Mari tried to calm herself down as she started her engine. Her parents usually fought in the privacy of their own home, not within earshot of customers. All she could think was that the failed camping trip must have really ticked her mother off. She had already been disappointed that the farthest away from home she could manage to get her husband was a tent in Tortoise Nation. Mari's father must have said something that had been the final straw.

Back at Lito Bueno's Mexican Restaurant, Mari got out of the car and made her way through the packed parking lot. Crowds of people stood around in clusters talking excitedly to each other.

"I heard the owner shouting," one woman said. "Any idea what's happening?"

"All I know is that the Ramirez family was up in Tortoise Nation the night that Soto fella died," said a man in a wet baseball cap. "This is the most excitement I've seen in a while."

"Danny Soto?" he woman waiting replied. "You have got to be kidding me. Is that why all of these people are here? I thought it was the soft taco special."

Mari did her best to hold her tongue. It was obvious that none of the people waiting to be seated knew that she was a Ramirez. It was difficult listening to townsfolk speaking poorly of her family, but she knew it was better to remain polite when working in the service industry. After a few seconds of silence. Mari heard shouting coming from the back office.

"There it is again," the woman commented. "So unprofessional."

"Excuse me," Mari said, forcefully cutting her way through the crowd.

The people waiting eyed her resentfully but got out of the way so she could pass. When Mari made it to the back of the restaurant, she found her mom and dad standing in the back office at about ten paces from each other as if they were in a stand-off. Alex, David, and Chrissy stood off to the side looking helpless.

"I've had it up to here with your cheapness," Mrs. Ramirez shouted. "You've always been cheap. When we were first married, you stocked up on ramen and tuna because you said it was all we could afford. I thought it would get better once we were established, but if it were up to you, we would still be eating cheap tuna three times a day."

"I can't help that the economy is the way that it is," Mr. Ramirez argued, pulling out a cigarette. "We're lucky to even have a restaurant that is still up and running. You should be thanking me for my cheapness."

"You never take risks, José," Mrs. Ramirez continued. "You've been scraping and saving for thirty years, and what for? It's time you spent some of that money on your family. Stop working so hard and enjoy the fruit of your labors. At least, take your wife somewhere more appealing than a run-down campground!"

"I bought us that new tent, didn't I?" Mr. Ramirez said defensively. "It wasn't even on sale. You didn't even say thank you for that. I'm tired of how ungrateful you've all become."

"Don't accuse me of being ungrateful," Mrs. Ramirez retaliated. "I know perfectly well how much you've sacrificed for this family, and I thank heaven for it every day of my life. I'm not mad *at* you, I'm mad *for* you. I'm mad because you haven't taken more than two days' vacation in thirty years. I'm mad because I think you could have a life outside of this restaurant if you would just let yourself. When you're on your deathbed, you're not going to say *I wish I had worked more hours at the restaurant—*"

"Oh, here we go," Mr. Ramirez muttered in an irritated voice.

"One day you'll wish you'd listened to me." Mrs. Ramirez crossed her arms.

"Is that a fact?"

For a moment no one spoke. Mrs. Ramirez was close to tears but had managed to hold them in.

"I'm not going to shut down the restaurant to take you somewhere fancy, Paula," Mr. Ramirez said as he sat down in his office chair. "Do you have any idea how much money we lose when we close?"

"Hire a manager." Mrs. Ramirez rolled her eyes.

"I have two sons and a daughter. Why would I do that?"

"Oh, José." Mrs. Ramirez shook her head in disappointment. "I've given up so much for this family and this restaurant. I deserve to be lounging on a tropical beach drinking Pina Coladas."

"Go, then," Mr. Ramirez responded in a tone of perfect indifference. "Nobody is stopping you."

"You cannot be serious, José!" Mrs. Ramirez shouted. "I'm sick of you taking me for granted." Untying her apron, she threw it on the desk in front of him. "I've had enough. I quit. I'm sure you won't even notice I'm gone."

Mrs. Ramirez turned to storm out, but Rick and a team of policemen blocked her path.

"Rick, what's going on?" Mari asked, wondering if one of the customers had called the police.

Rick looked apologetically at Mari and shook his head before turning to face her brothers.

"Alex and David Ramirez," he said, "I'm very sorry, but I'm here to take you in."

"What? Take them in where?" Mr. Ramirez narrowed his eyes as if Rick needed his permission to do his job.

"I'm sorry, Mr. Ramirez." Rick nodded at the policeman to his side. The policeman stepped forward with a pair of handcuffs. "I have to follow orders. Your boys are coming with me to the station."

CHAPTER ELEVEN

This was the first time a member of the Lito Bueno's Mexican Restaurant staff had been marched out in handcuffs. The arrest seemed to confirm everything that their customers had been whispering about them on the streets and in the dining room—that the Ramirez family was hiding something. Yet the line at the front entrance did not thin. If anything, it seemed to have grown when Mari finally left to return to her apartment.

After changing out of her work clothes, Mari called Rick. Tabasco sat eagerly at her feet, sensing that something was wrong. There was no answer, so she left him a message.

"My brothers didn't kill Danny, and I'm going to prove it," Mari stated.

"I'm on my way back to Tortoise Nation. Meet me at the Soto family lake house in one hour."

Mari leashed Tabasco, and together they made their way outside into the cool afternoon air. The rain had subsided into a light drizzle that fogged up the windows of her car, making it hard to see the road in front of her.

Mari felt certain that Maeve's disappearance was the key to the whole case. If she could find her, then she might have a shot at freeing Alex and David. And the place to begin looking was the Soto's lake house where she was almost certain Maeve had been the night of the murder.

Mari hit the steering wheel in frustration as she thought more about Danny Soto's case. She should have gone looking for Maeve when she saw the blue jacket lying on Danny's bed. She should have found the presence of a woman's jacket in Danny's room odd, but she hadn't thought about it. She had been distracted by the pictures on the wall and the surprise appearance of Leo Soto. In a case like this, there were simply too many pieces of the puzzle to keep track of. Also, some pieces didn't seem important at the time.

She parked in the vast parking lot at the entrance of Tortoise Nation's campground and walked back to the site where she and her mother had pitched tents the day before. From there she was able to retrace the route she and her brothers had taken through the woods back to the lake, gray as cold marble, where the lake house stood.

Mari had spent the drive rehearsing a speech in her head explaining to the Sotos why they should let her into their home. But when she arrived, she found the place deserted. A quick inspection of the garage out back revealed that both cars were gone. And although Tabasco barked as they approached the house, and Mari thought she saw a curtain fluttering in an upstairs window out of the corner of her eye, no one answered when she knocked on the door.

Wanting to be completely sure there was no one home, she knocked once, twice, even three times and waited. When enough time had passed, and there was still no response, she began scanning the perimeters of the house looking for a way in.

In the end, it was Tabasco who found it—a window on the lower level leading into the game room that had been left open just a crack. She thought it might have been this window that a couple of partyers had jumped out of the night before. That would explain why it was still open. Placing her hands underneath it, she lifted it up just enough to fit herself and Tabasco into the room. Then, taking a final glance around to make sure they weren't being watched, she rolled herself inside onto a leather sofa.

It was unlikely that Maeve had been in this room. If she had, surely one of the crowds of people who had been there the previous night would have told the police. But she took a quick look around before she left just to be sure. No one had bothered cleaning the place since last night. Pizza boxes still stood in the corner. They were filled with stale crusts and plastic containers of half-eaten marinara sauce. A single slice of vegetable pizza lay in the top box, and it took a supreme act of swiftness to lure Tabasco away from it.

She left the room and had just reached the second floor when she heard what sounded like muffled screams coming from down the hallway. *Calm down, Mari*, she told herself as she ran toward it. *It's probably just an animal.*

But as she got closer to the source, she felt sure no animal could have made that noise. That was a human voice. That was the sound of a woman sobbing. What was going on?

The noises came from Danny's room. The door was shut, but not locked. Not for the first time, Mari reminded herself that Rick was on his way. Rick should have been there minutes ago, but she couldn't stand around waiting for him, not when someone was in trouble on the other side of the door.

Mari bravely walked into the bedroom. It looked much the same as it had the night before, and it appeared to be empty. But Tabasco immediately ran to the closet door and raised himself up on his hind legs, scratching to get in.

Mari opened the door to find Maeve Rivers, gagged and bound. Immediately she bent down, tore off the duct tape over her mouth, and began untying the cords around her ankles and wrists.

"What on earth happened here?" she asked. Maeve offered no resistance to Mari's assistance. "Who did this to you?"

Maeve's breathing was short and panicky.

"I shouldn't say," she breathed. "No. I don't want to talk about it. I don't want him to hurt me!"

Mari gripped her shoulders in an effort to calm her. "Look, you don't have to worry. I won't let anyone hurt you. Who did this?"

"Leo," Maeve responded, tears flooding down her face. "He murdered Danny. His own brother! He murdered him, and then he kidnapped me to keep me from telling anyone what he had done."

CHAPTER TWELVE

Mari played a quick series of scenarios in her head. Maeve had been missing since Danny's death. The last people to see her before she disappeared were Mari and her brothers. And the jacket on Danny's bed suggested that she had been at the lake house possibly this whole time. How long had she been trapped in the closet? Had she been stuck there when Mari had found Danny's room and Leo had interrupted her? Had Leo interrupted Mari on purpose to stop her from discovering his secret?

She had so many questions to ask Maeve, but first, they needed to get Maeve to the police station. Mari pulled Maeve to her feet, and Maeve wobbled slightly like she hadn't stood in a while.

"It's okay," Mari said again, taking her by the shoulders. "I'm going to get you out of here. My car is parked at the campsite. I'm going to bring you into the station. I know your parents will be very happy to know that you're okay."

But this promise was quickly put to the test as Mari heard the sound of the front door being unbolted. A second later the door opened and Leo Soto entered the house.

Mari froze with her arm still tight around Maeve, every nerve alert. At the same moment, Leo paused in the doorway as if sensing the presence of someone else in the house.

"Listen," Mari breathed low in Maeve's ear. "When I say *run*, we're going to run, okay? We're going to run to the back door, and we're not going to stop until we get there."

She began counting to three, but it was already too late for that. Leo, having heard them whispering, set down his groceries and ran toward the staircase.

"Hey!" Leo shouted.

"Now!" Mari cried as she sprinted for the exit. Tabasco barked furiously. She flung herself against Leo as he stood at the base of the stairs looking shocked.

Mari had managed to push Leo just enough to send him stumbling backward into a porcelain vase that wobbled back and forth. As he tried and failed to catch the antique before it broke, Mari slipped past him with Tabasco in tow and dashed toward the back door.

She found Maeve waiting for her outside. It was late afternoon, and dusk was falling, accompanied by a light mist that made the surrounding woods look like it was full of shadows.

"What are we going to do?" Maeve asked with a hopeless look. "We can't possibly outrun him."

"No," Mari replied, looking toward the woods. "But we can lose him. Follow me. We'll get to my car in no time."

Together they ran from the clearing in the direction of a hill covered with tall pines and carpeted with damp leaves in varying shades of red and brown. Mari was already exhausted from trying to get out of the house, and she knew Leo would have the energy to spare. But she had wandered these woods long enough to know how confusing and disorienting they could be, especially as night was falling.

"We might get lost," she told Maeve. "But it's okay, as long as we lose Leo. If we keep running long enough, we're bound to find our way back to a campsite."

Maeve didn't look reassured by this information, but they continued to jog at a brisk pace for several minutes. After about fifteen minutes had passed, they were surrounded by silence. Mari looked back and realized that Leo was nowhere in sight. If he had attempted to chase after them, they had lost him.

And now they were alone in the woods.

Instinctively Mari began looking around for familiar landmarks. Luckily Maeve seemed to have spent hours wandering alone through Tortoise Nation and was able to lead them, in a few minutes, back to a muddy road that ran alongside the lake. As they walked, Mari attempted to question Maeve about her abduction.

"What was Leo thinking kidnapping you like that and leaving you in Danny's closet?" she asked her. More to the point, why hadn't the police thought to look there the night before? It was hard to believe they could have failed to search the bedroom of a man who had just been murdered.

"I don't know what he was thinking," Maeve said quietly. The tone of her voice suggested that she didn't particularly care to talk about it. "It's hard to figure out the thought process of a mad man."

"I know he was upset with Danny," Mari went on, "but I didn't get the sense that he hated him. Not enough to kill him, anyway. Brothers fight sometimes. That's pretty normal. Trust me, I know."

"Yes, but have you ever read the story of Cain and Abel in the Bible?" Maeve replied.

"My Abuela is the religious one."

The more Mari thought about that answer, the more she found it unsatisfying. This wasn't some primal murder if such a thing even existed. Yet Maeve clung to that explanation, repeatedly insisting that Leo's motives were out of jealousy.

"Some people are bad, Mari," she explained. "Leo is one of those people. I guess one of the only downsides of marrying into the Soto family." Maeve took a deep breath. "Look, I don't want to talk about it."

"I get it. I suppose you can save your story for the police."

"I just suffered a severe trauma," Maeve said, looking at Mari with tears in her eyes. "I would prefer not to have to talk about it ever again."

CHAPTER THIRTEEN

They kept walking as the woods darkened around them. Mari knew that Maeve was nervous, but she hadn't heard anything suspicious in a while. She was confident that they would make it back to her car without any problems. Maeve walked several paces ahead of her.

Mari was still thinking through the mystery of Leo's motivations when her phone buzzed. Mari's heart jumped. The last time she had checked her phone, she had no service. It was Rick calling.

"Perfect timing," Mari said, answering the call. She stopped walking, and Tabasco looked up at her. "You caught me at the only stop around here that gets cell service."

"Where are you?" Rick urgently asked.

"I've got Maeve," Mari responded, not entirely able to conceal the tone of triumph in her voice. "We're on the trail that circles the lake."

"Wait there," Rick replied. "I will be there soon to pick you two up."

"Okay," Mari agreed. "Listen, Rick, I found Maeve tied up in Danny Soto's closet. Maeve said it was Leo who did it to her. Leo is the murderer. He's the guy you're looking for."

Rick listened patiently until she had finished. "How did we miss that? Well, Maeve's story certainly helps your brothers, but there is still no way Leo killed Danny."

"Why not?" Mari asked. Up ahead, Maeve had paused and appeared to be listening closely.

"Because we have multiple witnesses placing Leo at the lake house all night," Rick explained. "And before that, Leo was spotted in town. We can account for his whereabouts every single hour of the day."

"He could have done a day earlier and dumped his body in the woods?" Mari suggested, though even she knew it was a stretch.

"I'm sorry, Mari, but the timeline doesn't add up." Rick paused for a moment to collect his thoughts. "Unless we can catch Leo in a lie, your brothers are still in deep water."

True to his promise, a few minutes later Mari saw headlights coming toward them down the path. Tabasco growled at the sight and Maeve shuddered.

"Let's keep walking," Maeve said with a tremble in her voice. "Please."

"But it's Rick," Mari responded. "He has come to get us."

"Fine." Maeve gulped.

It seemed to Mari like Maeve was becoming increasingly paranoid. But Mari couldn't imagine what it must have felt like to lose a loved one and then be trapped in a closet for who knows how long. Reminding herself to be patient, she hurried along behind Maeve and flagged the car down as it pulled up beside them. The door opened, and Rick stepped out.

"See?" Mari said to Maeve. "There is nothing to worry about. Officer Kinney will take care of us."

During the time they had been together, it sometimes felt like Maeve was holding herself together by a thread. When she saw Rick, she broke down completely. Collapsing against the side of the car, she was hardly able to speak.

"She's just been through a terrible experience," Mari said sympathetically. "I can't even imagine."

"I'm just … so glad it's finally over," Maeve managed to say. "If it weren't for you, Mar, there's no knowing what he might have done to me."

Maeve stumbled forward and hugged Mari, and Mari patted her gingerly on the shoulder. Then, turning to Rick, Maeve flung her arms around him and wrapped him in a warm embrace. Rick resisted at first, looking distinctly uncomfortable, but he eventually accepted her advance.

Then a number of things happened very quickly.

Before Mari really understood what was happening, Maeve pushed herself away from Rick and shouted.

"Get back against the car!" Maeve yelled. "I said get against the car!"

As Rick stepped back against the passenger-side door, Mari saw an object in Maeve's hand. Maeve waved Rick's gun in the air before pointing it at him. She had somehow managed to snag it from Rick's holster.

"Maeve," Mari said in a dazed voice. "What are you doing?"

"Put the gun down," Rick calmly stated.

"Maeve, put it down."

"Mari," Rick said, keeping his eyes on the woman in front of him, "this woman is *not* Maeve Rivers."

"What?" Mari questioned.

"Shut up," the woman shouted. "No more talking!"

"But if she's not Maeve ..." Mari said. She studied the woman as she pointed the gun at Mari. Tabasco growled. "Who are you?"

But instead of answering, the imposter gestured to the car. "Get against the car next to your friend. And keep hold of your dog. Don't make me shoot him too!"

Hastening to comply, Mari put her back against Rick's squad car.

"Just tell me who you are," Mari said, a mixture of curiosity and worry in her voice.

"I told you, I'm Maeve Rivers," the woman replied.

"I've seen pictures of Maeve," Rick responded. "You are not who you say you are. Maeve Rivers is missing, and I suspect that you have something to do with her disappearance. Where is she?"

"Get in the car, Mari," the woman demanded. "Now."

Mari hastily obeyed. The woman pointed her gun at Rick and forced him to give her his keys. Rick tossed them to her, and the woman jumped in the driver's seat and pushed on the gas. Before Mari knew it, she watched Rick and Tabasco in her side view mirror grow farther away from her. The woman claiming to be Maeve Rivers sped down the muddy road through potholes and around fallen branches.

Mari did her best to remain calm by focusing on the facts of the case. She was so close to getting the answers she had been searching for, and the feeling that her brothers stood a chance of walking free steadied her nerves as the car sped through Tortoise Nation.

"Just tell me," Mari said. "Who are you, really?"

The woman didn't answer.

"Did you kill Danny Soto?" Mari guessed. "Why would you do that?"

"Because he deserved it," the woman blurted out. "Danny Soto was a horrible person. I did the real Maeve Rivers a favor. I never wanted you to get involved, but when you started snooping around the lake house, you left me with no choice."

"Then the whole kidnapping—"

"You mean *my* kidnapping?" asked the woman with a small smile. "Yes, that was staged for you. I was searching through Danny's bedroom this afternoon when I saw you at the front door. I decided to set a trap by cracking open one of the downstairs windows and tying myself up in the closet."

"What are you planning to do with me then?" Mari asked though she had a feeling she wasn't going to like the answer.

"The only thing I really can do at this point," the woman answered. "You know too much. Now, shut up."

Thinking quickly, Mari realized that her best chance of escaping alive was now when the woman was focused on the road in front of her. Slamming herself against the woman's shoulder, Mari managed to push her far enough out of the driver's seat to grab hold of the steering wheel.

The car went flying off the road, and there was a dreadful moment where they seemed to be spinning around in circles. Mari wondered briefly if this was the last thing she was going to remember before she died. The car came to a sudden halt between two trees, narrowly missing both.

Taking advantage of the imposter's panic and disorientation, Mari opened her door and ran for her life.

"Don't make me do this!" came a voice from behind her. "I don't want to, but I swear I will."

She fired once.

The noise was deafening, but Mari kept running.

Another shot fired into the night.

"Get back here!" the woman called.

"Not in a million years," Mari muttered under her breath. "Not even my brothers are that stupid."

The sound of tires splashed through the mud, and a pair of headlights came into view. Mari let out a grateful sigh of relief. The car halted just in front of her. At first, Mari thought it was Rick and that he had somehow acquired another car with the help of the police. But then the door opened, and a man stepped out, holding a hunting rifle. It was Leo Soto.

"Your little game is over, Kelly," Leo said to the woman. "Drop your gun. You know I *will* shoot you."

"Make me!" Kelly shouted in the distance.

Mari stopped running and turned around, struggling to see through the thick darkness that was taking over the woods. There was a tense silence as she looked from Kelly to Leo. Both had their guns aimed at the other.

"You know, I have to admit," Leo said, "I almost didn't recognize you with blonde hair. I've seen a lot of terrible dye jobs, but yours is the worst. Blonde really isn't your color."

"Stop patronizing me," Kelly yelled. "You don't know anything about me!"

"But you did," Leo shouted back. "You and Danny were never a couple, and now you never will be."

Hot tears stung Kelly's cheeks as the enormity of her guilt seemed to press down on her. "I didn't … I didn't mean to kill Danny. That was never the plan."

"What did you do with Maeve?" Leo asked coldly.

"All I wanted," Kelly said, "was to take her place for the night. Just for one night. You have no idea how it feels to see the man you love with another woman. That should have been me.'"

"That is called jealousy," Leo replied. "We've all struggled with it, but that is no reason to kill someone."

"I just wanted him to see that he'd made a big mistake," Kelly argued. "Maeve wasn't right for him. He was supposed to be with me. Me!"

"So what?" Leo continued pulling the truth from Kelly's lips. "You thought you would show up at the lake house and Maeve and that Danny would play along? That's crazy."

"No, of course not." The expression on Kelly's face changed. Mari's eyes went wide as Kelly began showing her true colors. Crazy ones. "I tried talking to him, but all he cared about was his precious Maeve. *Where's Maeve? Oh, poor Maeve.* I don't even know her, and I'm already tired of her."

Mari was sure that Kelly was on the verge of some sort of breakdown.

"Put the gun down, Kelly," Mari said quietly. "The police are on their way, and they know what you've down. It's all over."

Before Kelly could decide what to do next, the sound of sirens rang through the air. The lights of a police car came into view, and Mari took a deep breath. Finally, the truth had come out and would soon set her brothers free.

CHAPTER FOURTEEN

"So the whole time we were talking to Maeve in the woods," Alex said as they left the police station, "it was really this other woman impersonating her?"

Mari nodded soberly, shielding her eyes against the morning sunlight. "Apparently, Kelly has a few mental health problems. She and Danny had dated back in high school, but Danny eventually broke things off when he met Maeve."

"Sounds terrifying," David chimed in. "This is why dating scares me."

"Everyone's terrifying when you get to know them," Alex commented. "So that was her plan then? She wanted to take Maeve's place? What a psycho."

"It wasn't very well thought out, I know," Mari replied. "On the day of the murder, Kelly dyed her hair blonde. It was the day of Maeve and Danny's anniversary, and she knew they would be celebrating up at the lake house. At least, that's what Rick told me." Mari cleared her throat as she thought through the details Rick had told her about Danny's murder. "I guess they fought. Danny ran into the woods looking for Maeve and Kelly ended up stabbing him with his own hunting knife."

"Yikes," Alex commented. "I'm never getting married. Some women don't know when to quit."

"Seriously?" Mari rolled her eyes.

"He's off of love at the moment because things with him and Jia Chun didn't work out," David added.

"Whatever." Alex shook his head. "Haven't you seen the way Mom and

Dad have been arguing? I don't want to be yelled at every day for the rest of my life."

Mrs. Ramirez had hung up her apron, and she still wasn't speaking to her husband. When Mari had last spoken to her over the phone, she told her she wasn't coming back to work until Mr. Ramirez agreed to leave the restaurant in the hands of his kids for a whole night and take her out on a date.

That night at the restaurant as the staff celebrated Alex and Danny's release from jail, Mr. Ramirez stood up and made an announcement.

"Having my boys back just reminds me that life is too short." Turning to face Mrs. Ramirez, he said, "Paula, I think it's time we went on a real vacation."

"What do you mean by real vacation?" Mari couldn't help but ask.

"I mean we're all going to the beach," her father stated.

David and Alex high-fived each other while Mrs. Ramirez wept quietly with satisfaction. Mari retreated to the kitchen and returned carrying a plate piled high with chicken soft tacos.

"So," Mari said as she took a seat at the table, "have we officially retired the Taco Danny special?"

"You wish, big sis," David replied with a smug look on his face. "We've been asked to keep it on the menu, by none other than Leo Soto himself. And of course, our customers love it."

Alex raised a solemn glass.

"To Danny," he said. "The worst and the best thing that's ever happened to our business."

"To Danny," said David and Mari.

BOOKS BY HOLLY PLUM

PATTY CAKES BAKE SHOP COZY MYSTERIES
Until Death Do Us Tart
For Butter Or For Worse
Something Bakes and Something Blue
Frying The Knot
Wedding Bells and a Body
Saying Pie Do . . . (Coming Soon)

MEXICAN CAFÉ COZY MYSTERIES
Murder Con Carne
Killer Salsa
Smothered In Lies
Rice, Beans, and Revenge
Crimes and Chimichangas
Soft Taco Murder

Thank you for your support! If you would like to know more about new releases and other fun things, sign up for my author newsletter by visiting my author page on Amazon.com.

Printed in Great Britain
by Amazon